FOOTPRINTS on SNOW

Seven Brave Women Who Shaped
the History of
the Northwest Mountains

JOAN BURTON

Archway Publishing books may be ordered through booksellers or by contacting:

Archway Publishing
1663 Liberty Drive
Bloomington, IN 47403
www.archwaypublishing.com
844-669-3957

ISBN: 978-1-6657-0662-9 (sc)
ISBN: 978-1-6657-0663-6 (hc)
ISBN: 978-1-6657-0661-2 (e)

Print information available on the last page.

Archway Publishing rev. date: 10/13/2021

CONTENTS

Why Tell These Stories?

I wrote this book to acknowledge mountaineering women who had made significant contributions, yet are not recognized as they should be. I knew some of them personally or shared time with them. For years I had been thinking, "If I don't tell these stories, who will ever tell them?" You get to decide whether their stories are important in Northwest mountaineering history, amazing stories worth telling.

Like Fay Fuller, the first time I climbed Mount Rainier was by the Gibraltar route. Park Service guides have not used that route for years.

I remember how steep the cliff looked, how it dropped rocks right down on us, and how I shuddered with fear as I crossed the Ledge. That drop-off below the Ledge was terrifying! Because I climbed on the same climbing route she used, I admire Fay Fuller even more for her courage and determination.

Polly Dyer and I took the Mountaineers Climbing Course together. I remember standing in line with her for rappelling practice at the Duwamish Piers. We discussed how apprehensive we felt about sliding down a rope over a wall, and soon, a cliff. Polly loved the wilderness and would work hard to preserve it, but she certainly didn't love climbing. Her accomplishments outweighed her dislike of climbing, but she had the determination to pass the Climbing Course. I admired her stubborn persistence in her fight to save wilderness beaches, forests, and mountains.

Louise Marshall was the leader of a group of intrepid housewives calling themselves the Happy Hikers. When my children were in school, I joined them. Once a week we followed her onto rural Snohomish County roads and trails. She was just starting *Signpost* magazine, and so we heard how she inquired about trail conditions by making phone calls each week, and then writing what she had learned in the next *Signpost* hiking bulletin. As far as we knew, publishing trail reports had never been done here before. Louise was an innovator. Out of the popularity of the magazine came the first hiking organization, the Washington Trails Association.

Pam Bobroff and I were friends in Mountaineers climbing days, but we renewed the friendship in her old age when she was suffering from multiple sclerosis and a spreading paralysis. When I visited her at the Foss Home, she would tell me about serving as a fire lookout during the war with her mother and grandmother. Because she missed the mountains so much, her caregiver and I drove her in a car to the North Cascades, and then pushed her in a wheelchair up the short, paved trail to Rainy Lake. Pam loved seeing an alpine lake and breathing mountain air once again.

You can see I am telling the stories of friends who loved Northwest mountains as I did. I can never forget them and their contributions to mountaineering and conservation. I hope you will enjoy and remember their stories too.

THE FIRST WOMAN TO CLIMB MOUNT RAINIER: HOW FAY FULLER, WEARING BLOOMERS, REACHED THE SUMMIT IN 1890

Mount Rainier. Photo by Gary Rose

It all started at a time when women were expected to stay home, when a young girl named Fay Fuller dreamed of climbing the biggest mountain in the Pacific Northwest.

Born in New Jersey in 1869, Fay Fuller moved to Tacoma, Washington when she was 12 years old. There she discovered beautiful mountains and wilderness around her. She graduated from high school when she was just 15 and took a job teaching in the small town of Yelm, southeast of Olympia. Women in the 19th century still wore long full skirts. Hardly any had finished university training, which is why she was already working, teaching school at her young age. She probably taught all the grades represented by her students.

Because her father was the editor of a local newspaper called *Every Sunday*, she had grown up reading news and writing her own articles. She was especially fond of stories about mountaineering and climbing.

Philemon B. Van Trump, one of the first to climb the mountain, came to her school one day and told her rapt students about climbing Mount Rainier in 1870. Fay was excited by his story and became determined to try to climb it herself

Mount Rainier. Photo by Gary Rose

She made her first attempt in 1887, when she got to about 8,800 feet, the approximate level of Anvil Rock. Without proper equipment, she could go no higher. She gazed across the valleys to the Tatoosh Range and the big white mountains in Oregon. Seeing the spectacular views from there just made her want to do more and go higher. She really wanted to climb all the way to the top of the mountain where the views would be so spectacular. She didn't know if she had a chance. She knew she couldn't do it alone.

Despite disapproval from people in the community, who thought a woman had no place climbing the mountain, she promised herself she would try again to "climb to the summit of the great peak."

Fortunately, celebrity climber Van Trump had become her friend and encouraged her. In the summer of 1890, Mr. and Mrs. Van Trump invited Fay to go along with them and their 10-year-old daughter Christine on a camping trip to a hillside below Mount Rainier and to join a climbing party the next day.

That Friday night as they ate their supper, Mr. Van Trump told them the origin of the name of their campsite. When the pioneer Longmire family had climbed upward from the Longmire hotel and hot springs into the alpine meadows at 5,000 feet, Virinda Longmire had asked, "What is the name of this beautiful place?" Someone must have replied, "It has no name." "Surely," she remarked, "then it must be Paradise." Fay smiled, thinking that the name for the Paradise meadows around them was so appropriate.

Paradise alpine meadow. Photo by Gary Rose

In those days, when she went hiking and climbing, Fay wore what was supposed to be a climbing costume, made up by her dressmaker, which was a blue flannel bloomer suit, a loose blouse with many pockets, heavy leather boy's shoes, warm mittens, goggles, and a small straw hat. Her alpenstock (walking stick) had been crafted by a blacksmith from a shovel handle. Some people told her later that the costume was immodest because it was casual and sporty. But Fay found it hot, cumbersome, and a hindrance to moving.

What do you think of it? Would you want to go mountain climbing in this outfit?

Fay Fuller, circa 1890. Mount Rainier National Park Archives and Museum Collection

The next day, Philemon Van Trump introduced Fay to a party of four men and another woman who planned to conquer Rainier. In August of 1890, no white woman had ever climbed the mountain, and, as far as anyone knew, no person had ever spent the night on the summit. That was the year climbers first realized they could do that, thereby avoiding afternoons when falling rock and other dangers are more likely to occur.

The group planned to leave the next morning and camp overnight in the crater at the summit. Fay told them of her dream to climb Mount Rainier too. When they saw how eager she was, they invited her to join them.

At last!

Fay was trembling when she told them "yes." She wanted to see the sunset and sunrise from the top. What else would she see? Maybe Puget Sound and the Olympic Mountains. Maybe even farther!

She resolved to climb until exhausted. She promised them and herself she would not require help, because if she couldn't do it on her own, she didn't deserve to reach the summit. Even if that meant jumping across crevasses, she would try.

Unfortunately, the man with the only camera dropped it, breaking the lens. There are no photos of this group of climbers.

Crevasses on Rainier glacier. Photo by Bob and Ira Spring

The next morning, they started up from their Paradise high camp. The streams and creeks were frozen, so they had no water to drink on the way, but Fay had filled her Uncle Sam's canteen the night before. Breakfast was dried prunes and raisins, which she chewed as they climbed. She reported she had put a good supply of chocolate into a pocket for a treat. But when the sun came out and warmed her back, what do you suppose happened to the chocolate?

The other woman climber, Edith Corbett, began to complain of a queasy stomach, which slowed her down. The climbers couldn't wait for her, and she turned back. Later, people would say it was immodest of Fay, the only woman left in the party, to climb with four men. But she didn't worry about that at the time.

Ice Chute of Gibraltar. Photo by Gary Rose

After seven hours they reached the base of an enormous 900-foot cliff called the Rock of Gibraltar. Fay was terrified at the sight of it. Their way led across the rock on a down-sloping ledge to the other side of the rock. Hundreds of feet below lay the Nisqually Glacier. One slip would send them sliding down to the ice. One of the party accidentally dropped his pack and it flew over the edge to the glacier below. Though they carried a rope, they did not tie into it, since they believed it would endanger everyone roped together if one of them slipped. Instead, they attached it on either side of the Gibraltar Ledge, so they had a fixed line to hold on to as they crossed.

Climbers on Gibraltar Ledge, Peggy J. Printz watercolor, from a photo by Dee Molenaar

Above, loose rocks had frozen into ice, but every so often some would melt out of the ice and hurl themselves down upon them. As the day went on, bright sunlight melted the ice and more rocks tumbled out of their positions. The party crossed the ledge as quickly as they could and their leader chopped steps upward into the ice.

Fay was out of breath because of the elevation, the speed with which they had moved, and from pure fear. They paused on top of Gibraltar at 12,000 feet for a brief rest. They were discouraged when It looked to them as though the summit was still a long way ahead.

By then they had gained enough elevation that they could see other mountains and glaciers below, but she wasn't sure of all their names at the time. She knew that the peaks directly below were the Tatoosh Range. Their spires had seemed big and imposing when they started up from Paradise but had dwindled in size as she and her companions climbed higher and above them. The big white mountains on the horizon to the south were Mount St. Helens and Mount Adams, volcanoes like Rainier, and still further south, Mount Hood and Mount Jefferson.

Mouth of Rainier crevasse with Mount Adams in distance. Photo by Bob and Ira Spring

The crevasses ahead looked fearful and difficult to cross. Some of them were narrow enough to jump, but for others they had to find snow bridges that were safe to cross. When they peered down into the crevasses, the cracks seemed to extend downward with blue shadows for hundreds of feet. As the party went on, Fay noticed she had to stop for breath for every 15 feet she traveled.

At 4:10 on Sunday afternoon, they stood on the rim of the crater. It was tilted like a giant saucer and the heat of the steam caves below had melted the snow on the rim, which was mostly warm, wet gravel. The heat came from the live volcano beneath them. The wind was blowing so hard they could barely stand up, and it was bitterly cold. Their summit view was disappearing into clouds.

Rainier Summit Crater Rim. Photo by Bob and Ira Spring

Still, they had to continue onward to the summit. At 4:30 on August 10, 1890, they reached Columbia Crest, the high point on the other side of the saucer-like crater. It was a heavenly moment. No one spoke because it was impossible for any of them to express their excitement and joy. Below them was a magnificent panorama. The giant Nisqually, Cowlitz, and Wilson glaciers and their rivers spread out into the valleys and prairies beyond. Wisps of cloud drifted below. The forests extending up to the rocks and snow looked like folds of green velvet. On the skyline were ranges of other mountains in every direction. In her later writing, Fay tried to describe the beauty of the scenery. She said it was difficult to put into words because the view seemed to be speaking to their souls. Do you wonder how the mountains could speak to the soul?

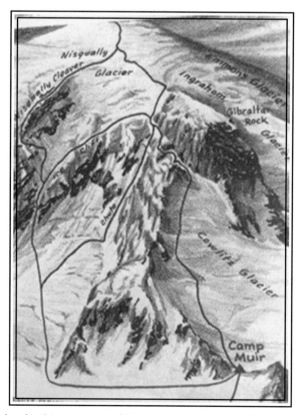

South Side climbing route of Mount Rainier. Map by Dee Molenaar

The wind was so strong they had to find shelter inside the crater. They crowded into steam caves and prepared themselves for the night. Mount Rainier is an active volcano. It has hot steam caves because the heart of the mountain is alive with hot volcanic magma, not buried very far below the surface of the crater.

Some of the party soaked their feet in whiskey they had brought along for that purpose. No one had much appetite, which was just as well since they were too tired to cook. The sulfurous odor of the steam made Fay feel slightly sick.

It was hard to sleep in the steam caves, alternating between scalding heat and icy winds. Fay watched meteors in the sky, listening to the sounds of what she later called "God's music" made by the avalanches and the constant wind. The sun set, but they were so cold and tired they didn't see it. The next morning, they knew they needed to start down early to avoid the rockfall in hot sun on the Gibraltar Ledge, so they packed up and were under way again by 8:30 am.

Sardine Can with Climbers' Record, Left on Rainier Summit, Peggy J. Printz watercolor

The party left a sardine can in the crater filled with scraps of paper bearing their names. The next day more summit climbers found hairpins in the crater which, they laughingly declared, proved that a woman had been to the summit. (Hairpins were like metal bobby pins, essential to holding women's long hair in place.) The descent was dangerous, as they faced more of the same dangers from rockfall along the Gibraltar Ledge. A new threat emerged: temporary painful damage to the climbers' eyes from the sun reflecting on snow. It was part of the price they had to pay to climb Mount Rainier. Their recovery at the Paradise base camp took five days before they felt well enough to go home again.

The climb changed Fay's life. For years afterward she fought to make Mount Rainier a national park. She wrote stories for her father's newspaper and spoke to community groups to help persuade important people to make that a reality. In 1899 that dream came true too. Mount Rainier National Park was established as the fifth U.S. national park.

She was active in developing a Pacific Northwest climbing community and helped found the Washington Alpine Club and the Mazamas mountaineering club in Portland, Oregon. Fay Peak near Mowich Lake in the national park was named for her.

Fay left teaching and became a journalist. She often said she believed the love of beautiful Mount Rainier can cure and heal most of the personal problems and pains we suffer.

Climbing Mount Rainier was one of the most inspiring and influential experiences in her life. Her achievement has motivated countless other women to follow in her footsteps.

Fay Fuller, date unknown, courtesy Dee Molenaar, *The Challenge of Rainier*

Spring photos courtesy Spring Trust for Trails www.springtrailtrust.com.

THE MOTHER OF THE PACIFIC CREST TRAIL: HOW CATHERINE MONTGOMERY'S IDEA BECAME A MAJOR HIKING ROUTE

Stretching from northern Washington to southern California, the Pacific Crest Trail sweeps across summits, undulates around glacial lakes and dips into valleys in some of North America's most majestic scenery. This trail was conceived in the mind of a Washington woman hiker almost a century ago.

Although she didn't set out with this goal, she connected several thoughts to come up with the concept. She spent a lot of energy promoting her idea, and she was fortunate enough to live long enough to see her vision realized. Tens of thousands of hikers, backcountry skiers and snowshoers enjoy parts or all of the trail every year. It's become a legend, a quest and a place to enjoy the spectacular scenery of the far Western mountains.

Catherine Montgomery loved mountains. Any mountains. Wherever she was, she looked for trails and the foothills they could take her to. She called it *tramping*. She enjoyed tramping on trails around her new home. A founding member of the teacher's college that would become Western Washington University, she had come all the way across the United States from Prince Edward Island north of Maine to Bellingham, Washington, to serve as a founding professor of education. Mountains surrounded her, and she was delighted to be able to begin to explore the North and Central Cascades. A bonus was the sight of actual volcanoes she saw on the skyline.

Pacific Crest Trail Sign in the Snow. Photo by Peggy J. Printz

Catherine and her best friend, Ida Baker, another professor, spent their weekends and summers together wandering amidst the beautiful mountains of the North Cascades. Sometimes they went backpacking to remote areas. There were no maps or guidebooks, so they found their way by themselves. They wore ankle-length bloomers because that was what women hikers wore in in the wilderness in those days.

In 1924 she discovered an article in a national monthly magazine *American Forestry* titled "The Appalachian Trail from Maine to Georgia by Foot Trail—A little Hike of 2,000 Miles Along the Skyline of the Appalachian Ranges." Catherine read it avidly and was fascinated.

Hikers had devised and built a trail that took them from the northern tip of New England all the way to the Deep South in Georgia.

That knowledge rapidly led to her brainstorm. The mountains she and Ida had explored were part of a natural divide—just like the Appalachian peaks and ridges. Hikers here could follow the crest of the Western mountains just as they did back east. Why not design a new trail from Mexico to Canada?

Puzzled about how to proceed, she told nobody about her idea. Ida Baker had died several years earlier. The concept continued to germinate in Catherine's mind.

One morning nearly two years later, Catherine was listening to Joseph Hazard, a member of the Seattle Mountaineers Club, who was trying to convince her to buy his textbooks for the college. He had also traveled to Bellingham to speak that night to the Mount Baker Club, the local mountaineering club. Suddenly she interrupted him.

"Do you know what I was thinking about as we sat here, Mr. Hazard?

"I was hoping you were considering buying my books, Miss Montgomery."

"Oh that. Of course, I will. I consider them the best. I still do.

But why don't you Mountaineers do something big for Western America?"

"Just what do you have in mind, Miss Montgomery?"

"A long, winding trail along the crest of the mountains with mile markers and shelter huts from Mexico to Canada, like the Appalachian Trail in this magazine. I have been reading about that trail on the east coast. We should have one here like it running down the west coast."

Joseph Hazard was speechless, as he looked at the magazine story she handed him and he smiled. He knew a great idea when he saw one. He took that idea and the magazine with its pictures to his lecture at the Bellingham Mountaineers that very night. Everyone there liked the idea and decided to work toward making it a reality.

Catherine Montgomery was delighted. Though she kept her academic job, she often joined promoters to help plan for the trail and its construction. She and her colleagues lobbied hard for the funds to make it happen.

Mountaineers members in Seattle, Tacoma and Olympia also agreed and banded together. They organized to raise money to buy the land and clear it for a long, winding trail along the crest of the coastal mountains. Completing the entire trail took many years, but adventuring athletes soon began to hike along the half-finished trail. After it was completed and as the years went by, the trail became enormously popular and beloved by long distance "through hikers." Today's hikers try to cover it all in one season, starting in Mexico in early spring and reaching Canada in October just as winter snows begin. Catherine Montgomery probably never did get to hike the trail, but she contributed money to build it and was an influential supporter of the effort.

Women hikers near Seattle circa 1920. Photo courtesy Cindy McRoberts

Catherine Montgomery lived to be 90, long enough to know that the Pacific Crest Trail as she had dreamed it had become a reality. She was aware that it was a valued treasure. She might have also realized that "through hikers" would compete with one another to be the fastest travelers along the trail.

She had saved enough money on her professor's salary to build a nature interpretive center at Federation Forest. But her part in the visualization and creation of the Pacific Crest Trail had been forgotten by many. In 2010 she was inducted into the Western Washington University's Women's Hall of Fame which reversed that omission.

Federation Forest Sign. Photo by Joan Burton

At that gathering, Catherine Montgomery was named the "Mother of the Pacific Crest Trail." And that's how we remember her today.

A CANADIAN WHO LOVED MOUNTAINS AND WANTED TO BE FIRST: PHYLLIS MUNDAY

Phyl Munday was a Canadian woman who loved mountains and mountain climbing. She lived near the British Columbia Coast Range, so she looked at mountains that inspired her every day. Her father was a champion tennis player, who wanted his athletic daughter to play tennis. He said to her, "When you've climbed one mountain, why isn't that enough?" Phyl retorted, "When you've played one game, why isn't that enough?"

She began climbing in 1910 when women wore bloomers. She learned to climb with a friend, Annette Buck. They couldn't be seen in public wearing bloomers, so they hid them under long skirts until they reached the trail, where they could remove and hide the skirts. They had to find them and put them back on before they could return home on the streetcar.

By the end of World War I she was volunteering in the New Westminster Hospital near Vancouver when she met Don Munday, a wounded veteran who also loved mountains. They were married in 1920 and even after the arrival of a baby girl, they went climbing every chance they got, taking Edith with them, her head peeking out from inside their packs. Not surprisingly, she grew up to be fearless in the wilderness. She said of her childhood that "she might have taken second place to a mountain."

Climbers who wanted to travel to the British Columbia mountains found their way made difficult by constant bad weather and lack of roads or trails. Most of the peaks had never been climbed. Without many roads, climbers could only get to the mountains by water. But Phyl and Don Munday couldn't stay away from them.

One day they were out in a small boat on Knight Inlet gazing at the mountains when Phyl saw a giant unknown mountain on the horizon. It looked as though it was floating above the water. It was larger and higher than any mountain they had seen so far. They named it "Mystery Mountain". Phyl became obsessed with their Mystery Mountain and they tried again and again to climb it. Sixteen times they tried! They came close several times, but a few times they had to turn back to meet the boat that had brought them to the base of the mountain, or other times bad weather forced them back. She desperately wanted to make the first ascent, but someone else ultimately did that. Phyl was a good sport. The mountain was ultimately named Mount Waddington, elevation 13,186 feet, the highest peak in the British Columbia Coast Range.

Mount Waddington, Phyllis's Mystery Mountain.
Photo by Gary Rose

In 1924 the president of the Alpine Club of Canada gave Phyl and Don Munday "permission" to try to make the first ascent of Mount Robson. Most everyone they knew thought it was too difficult for a woman climber and they discouraged her.

It was technically challenging, but Phyllis and her friend Annette Buck and a group of others conquered it anyway. They used only ice axes and ropes to make their way up its steep ice cliffs. Phyl said "Without a professional guide I had scaled as difficult ice walls before, but never with such an excess of nothingness under my heels, or so much impending above."

When she was climbing the last short face, a fellow climber reached out a hand to her and said, "There, lady. You are the first woman on top of Mount Robson." Summiting the second highest peak in the Coast Range was the realization of a dream for her.

Mount Robson. Photo by Gary Rose

Phyl Munday outlived Don by decades. She became a beloved public figure in the climbing community and people asked her to teach and guide climbing parties in the BC Coast Range. In her lifetime she was called the Grand Dame of the Coast Mountains. Phyl climbed at least 100 peaks, and a third of them were first ascents.

In 1998 the Canadian government honored her with a postage stamp bearing her picture.

Postage stamp of Phyllis Munday. Photo by Ira Spring

DEFENDER OF NORTHWEST MOUNTAIN WILDERNESS: POLLY DYER

Polly Dyer was not born in the Northwest, but after she had come to live here, she fell in love with its mountains, ancient forests, and untouched natural beauty. She spent her life fighting for the trees in old growth forests and the great volcanoes and mountain ranges surrounding Puget Sound. She wanted to save the natural world from development and destruction. She believed that logging forests that had grown over thousands of years was a crime against future wilderness lovers.

When she first came to the Northwest, she took a Seattle Mountaineers mountain climbing course, but she didn't particularly like climbing. Sliding down a rope on a rock cliff did not thrill her, and crossing steep snow slopes with an ice axe was scary. But she loved the thousand-year-old trees. She loved the volcanoes and chains of mountains and high alpine lakes. She loved the fragile mountain meadows. She could see that logging, dam building, and road building would damage or destroy the natural world she loved. The damage would be irreversible.

What could she do to stop them? Destruction was already beginning. Forests in the mountains and foothills looked as though moths had nibbled at their carpets. Polly wanted to let people know how important it was to save and protect the Cascades and Olympics from loggers and developers. Olympic National Park was already threatened by people who wanted to shrink its boundaries so they could gain access to cut the big trees.

Road builders wanted to put a scenic highway along the ocean coast so people could see the ancient forest and beaches without ever leaving their cars. Polly knew a highway like that would damage the ocean beaches forever. Trash would be thrown out windows, ocean beaches would be littered, and the roaring sound of trucks and cars would spoil the silence of the forest.

There was something she could do. She could lead a protest walk with a famous person, Supreme Court Justice William O. Douglas, along that beach. Reporters and photographers would follow them and tell their readers about the wilderness ocean beach.

In 1958 Polly Dyer and Justice Douglas walked 22 miles of the roadless Pacific Ocean beach from Lake Ozette to Rialto Beach. Seventy other walkers and reporters walked with them. They camped in the driftwood and watched the enormous waves. Justice Douglas pointed out how fragile the beach was, and they saw its beauty for themselves. The reporters wrote stories about why the ocean beach should not have a highway next to it. And none was built. Polly had her first triumphant success.

Polly Dyer (2nd left) and William O. Douglas (right) on hike protesting proposed coastal highway, Olympic National Park, August 19, 1958. (NCCCC *Wild Cascades,* Winter 2017. Courtesy MOHAI (Image No. PI 86.5.23791.1)

She joined the Sierra Club and other outdoor groups. She led a Girl Scout troop, although she had no children of her own. She said, "We didn't waste any time on crafts. We went hiking and camping every chance we got." The girls remembered what she had said about helping to save the wilderness, and years later, inspired by Polly's influence, one of the girls came to a public hearing to advocate for protecting wilderness.

Tree "pirates" would sneak into the Olympic National Forest at night to cut trees to sell to the mills in Port Angeles. Even just one of the enormous thousand-year-old trees would be worth a great deal of money. Local people didn't turn in the tree cutters to the Forest Service because they too were secretly logging in the forest.

Polly helped to organize the Olympic Park Associates, a community group that fought illegal logging. Forest Service employees called the practice "salvage logging," excusing the cutting as a way to protect forests from insects or disease. But members of the Olympic Park Associates believed that term was just an excuse for the illegal loggers to cut as many trees as they could before they were caught. In 1956 two rangers quietly approached Polly Dyer and another wilderness supporter, Phil Zalesky, and asked them to report what was going on, without endangering their own jobs.

Polly knew that the governor of Washington wanted to shrink Olympic Park boundaries and to ignore the logging of the National Forest. He had established an Olympic Park Review Committee. Its purpose was to report on pirate logging of timber. Polly was not named to the Review Committee.

But a surprising thing happened. The chairman and the secretary couldn't attend the meeting, and they asked Polly to attend in their places and to take minutes. She attended, but she also stood up and spoke out in that meeting to protect the park and the trees.

Next, the Olympic Park Associates called the Director of the National Park Service Conrad Wirth to ask him to help them stop salvage logging. Polly Dyer was at the meeting with him. She took minutes, writing in shorthand in a notebook on her knee. Conrad Wirth said there would be no more logging in the national park. The president of the Olympic Park Associates sent the minutes to the Director. He said, "Yes, I guess I did say that. I didn't know I was being recorded." Because of his statement, he was forced to change the national park policy.

Today thanks to Polly's efforts, we can still see and enjoy Olympic old growth in the Hoh Rain Forest and elsewhere in nearby meadows and mountains.

In 1964 the national US Wilderness bill which became the Wilderness Act was proposed. Here is what Polly suggested in her letter of support for the bill.

"The Wilderness Bill's provisions will do a number of important and necessary things in behalf of the nation's present and future wild places and for its citizens who look for, or merely like to know that such sanctuaries exist. Wilderness cannot and should not wear a dollar sign. It is a priceless asset, which all the dollars man can accumulate, will not buy back. Some forest, which is commercially operable, has as much right to be kept primeval as the forest of non-commercial value."

She also contributed a phrase to the words of the Wilderness Act itself.

"A wilderness, in contrast with those areas where man and his own works dominate the landscape, is hereby recognized as an area where the earth and its community of life are untrammeled by man, where man himself is a visitor who does not remain." Polly suggested the phrase "untrammeled by man." She was proud of that contribution for the rest of her life.

Turning next to the North Cascades, Polly wanted to save the entire region in a national park. She wanted to include not only the big peaks, such as Mount Baker, Mount Shuksan and Glacier Peak, but the whole range of other mountains in the range, from the Canadian border to Snoqualmie Pass.

The new national park was planned, but Polly's vision did not prevail. The final park did not include the big peaks, nor the area she wanted to protect around the Skagit River. Some of the peaks were instead named as parts of a National Recreation Area, and others became the Mount Baker and Glacier Peak Wilderness areas. The other recreation area includes parts of the Skagit River, Ross Lake, Ross Dam and part of Lake Chelan. When Seattle City Light wanted to raise Ross Dam to provide more power and to flood more area around Ross Lake, Polly helped in the fight that defeated that plan.

Polly fought for passage of the Washington State Wilderness Act in 1984. This gave even more protection to undeveloped forest lands in the state. As president of the Olympic Park Associates, Polly worked for removal of the dams on the Elwha River.

At the end of her life Polly Dyer was still fighting to expand the North Cascades National Park to include more priceless North Cascades wilderness. Never a mountain climber or a skier, Polly Dyer was instead a heroic spokesman for the mountains and forests of Northwest wilderness. Because of her vision, much of the majesty of the forests and peaks of western Washington has been preserved for us today.

Polly Dyer on her 90th Birthday.
Photo by Karl Forsgaard, courtesy NCCC and *Wild Cascades* Magazine

V

PAM'S SUMMER IN THE FIRE LOOKOUT: PAM OLMSTED BOBROFF

Pam's friends were discussing their upcoming summer vacations. Pam's plans were the best of all. When she told the other 13-year-olds what she and her mother and grandmother were planning to do, they could barely believe her. Not one of her girlfriends was going to spend the summer in a fire lookout. In fact, not one had ever even been to a fire lookout.

Pam, Pam's mother, and her grandmother would be a team. Grandma was going to be the cook and woodchopper, Mother would scan the skies for enemy aircraft and watch for smoke starts of forest fires, and Pam was assigned to carry water from the spring in buckets and raise and lower the flag above their cabin. In wartime 1943 they would be the first and only three-generation fire lookout team in the USA.

They would live their lives at 5,200 feet on top of Suntop Mountain just north of Mount Rainier. There would be no radio to give them news or play music because they were too far from radio signals. Pam wouldn't be able to talk to her friends, because they were only allowed to use the telephone for calling in reports of fires or enemy planes. Their mail would be delivered to them by a Forest Service employee along with food supplies, but they didn't know when either would reach them.

The family team was getting ready to leave Seattle in mid-June for about three months. They needed to go as soon as school was out. Snow in the high country would be melting and the trail would be clear. Mother and Grandmother were packing cooking utensils and pots and pans the previous lookout might not have left behind. Their personal gear and the cooking tools were all going into big duffel bags to be carried on the backs of donkeys. They expected the views to be spectacular, so they were also packing a camera and rolls of film.

Pam said goodbye to her friends and gathered up her winter sweaters, ski pants, jackets, hats, and mittens. It seemed strange to be packing for cold and snow in June. Her friends laughed as they told her of the beach picnics she would miss, which she would have enjoyed. But Pam didn't care. She was going to live in a mountain meadow on top of a mountain for three months. If there was snow along the trail and around their cabin, it would be an adventure. She felt lucky!

At last, they were off, riding in Grandma's old pickup truck. They left Seattle very early in the morning because of the length of the trail they would hike up to the lookout. They would need to spend most of the day hiking alongside Forest Service pack animals carrying their gear. They reached the ranger station in Enumclaw just as the sun was coming up. The three transferred their duffel bags to a Forest Service truck, which also carried two pack donkeys named Silas and Sarah.

Pam got to ride in the back with the donkeys and feed them handfuls of hay to keep them contented. Grandma and Mother rode up front with the ranger, Mike, who drove up a steep winding dirt road to the trailhead. Pam guessed her mother was discussing how to use the Osborne Fire Finder with him. She had taken a class about this Forest Service tool to find and identify forest fires, but she was still reviewing it in her mind. She also had in her pocket little card silhouettes of enemy planes they might see and if so, which she would report to the Forest Service.

Magnificent Mount Rainier appeared to play peekaboo in places where the trees had been cut down. Known to locals as "The Mountain," it looked close enough that Pam wanted to get out of the truck and climb it.

"Okay, everybody out here," said Mike as he came to an abrupt stop at the trailhead. Pam hopped off the tailgate and joined in the loading of the duffel bags onto the donkeys' backs. The pack animals seemed accustomed to the process and stood patiently as more and more weight was added to their loads. Pam carried only a small daypack with snacks, a sweater, a bottle of water, and sunglasses. Mother and Grandmother had small daypacks of their own. Suddenly Pam wondered what they had forgotten, what they would miss. Surely this wasn't everything they would need for three months? She patted the neck of Silas, the closest donkey, and he gave a soft bray, which made them all laugh. The trailhead sign declared: Suntop Mountain, elevation 5,271 feet. Although it was still early, they would need the rest of the day just to get up to the lookout.

The three women changed into hiking boots, drank water from their Thermos bottles, and started up the trail. Mother advised Pam to take her time, and not rush. Mike was coming along to help them unpack and get situated at the lookout. He urged Silas and Sarah to get started.

Before they had gone far, the trail took them to the banks of the White River. Pam could see that it was indeed white. When she asked why the rushing water was not clear, Mike explained that it was full of ground up rock from the glacier. Because there was no bridge, they were going to have to ford the river. Pam certainly did not want to wade it. Mike said they would take turns riding on the donkey Silas's back across the rapids. They unloaded his duffel bags and Pam jumped up on his back. Silas seemed used to this routine. He strode through the rushing river confidently and Pam clung tight to his mane, talking to him all the way across. Mother and Grandma followed on separate trips.

After that the trail was long, steep and winding. At lunch time they stopped to eat the sandwiches they had brought with them. The donkeys seemed glad to stop, too, and munched on forest flowers alongside the trail. Pam was glad to rest, but it seemed there was still a long way to go. The good news was that the east side of Mount Rainier was coming into view more often. It was so beautiful Pam felt a new rush of energy whenever she saw it.

Would they be able to reach the lookout before dark? In June the days are long, and they had believed they would be there by dinnertime, long before dark. Now Pam wasn't so sure they would. The donkeys weren't the problem. They were moving evenly and smoothly. But Pam was tired and becoming exhausted. She sat down on the edge of the trail to take deep breaths. *Wouldn't it be nice to ride on Silas's back?* she thought. No, that wasn't in the. plan. The pots and pans jangled in the duffel bags as if to tell her so. The donkeys didn't need any more weight.

By 4:00 they emerged from the forest into subalpine meadows and more sweeping views of Mount Rainier. Virginia told Pam the huge ice cliff they were gazing at was called the Willis Wall. At last, they saw the lookout cabin itself perched on a high point. Clouds behind it capped the mountain, but they were only a few minutes from their summer home, as Pam thought of it, halfway to heaven. They had arrived.

Swiftly Grandma, Mike, and Mother unloaded the weary donkeys, and fumbled through the gear for two cans of spaghetti, their dinner. It seemed they were equally tired and hungry. Grandma fired up the two-burner camp stove, Pam found a bucket and made her way to the spring for water, and Mike started a campfire from the chunks of wood stacked by the cabin steps. He planned to eat with them, go over the Osborne Fire Finder rules and expectations with Mother one last time, then spend the night on the floor in his sleeping bag and get up early to start back down. As they devoured the last of the pot of spaghetti, a sunset reflected its colors on the snowbanks nearby. Clouds were turning lavender and purple. The temperature was plunging, and it was time for bed. She didn't care what time it was—Pam was ready.

Pam spread out her sleeping bag on a cot in the crowded one-room lookout and decided she would put her things away tomorrow. Mother and Mike were quietly reviewing the fire finder and how to call in a report on the two-way radio if she saw something suspicious. Pam fell asleep listening to their murmuring. She thought she heard him say that this lookout had never before been staffed by a woman. Not one woman, Pam thought to herself with a smile--- three!

In the night she heard a strange sound that wakened her, like a bird of prey calling out, but it didn't last long, and she dropped off again. She heard the wind come whistling down from the glaciers and blow through the alpine fir trees. When she woke up, she was the only one awake, but as she stepped out of the cabin, she saw Ranger Mike, getting the donkeys ready to leave. He whispered that he didn't need any breakfast, he would munch something on the trail down and leave them alone.

Pam, suddenly curious about enemy planes, asked him if any had been seen yet in the Snoqualmie National Forest. No, he told her, but that didn't mean they weren't there. He urged her to help her mother watch the skies for planes and the forest for smoke, or smoldering fires. He suggested that they look for at least 10 minutes out of every hour of daylight. *Oh dear,* she thought. That wouldn't leave her much time for exploring, but nevertheless, Pam promised him that she would help. Mike waved her a goodbye and said casually that he would be back in two weeks with the mail and a resupply of food.

Pam looked closely at the nearby snowbanks and noticed shoots of blueberry bushes poking their way upward through the crusty snow. Heather and white avalanche lilies were also struggling to reach the light. The flowers seemed to be trying to bloom even though their stems and roots were still buried in ice. That was brave of them, she thought. Would the bushes bear blueberries they could eat before she, Mother, and Grandma had to go down at the end of summer? She hoped so.

Pam decided to help make the pancakes for breakfast before Grandma got up. Back inside, she found the bag of flour mix and some eggs and fresh clean water in the bucket she had just dipped out of the nearby spring. There was a recipe on the bag, but Pam just poured and stirred until she was satisfied the batter was the right thickness. She had done this before at home. Grandma would be so pleased with her help, she was sure.

Grandma was surprised, all right, but when she heard Pam pouring and stirring, she got up in a hurry and made a few improvements to the pancake batter. They were hungry and devoured all the pancakes as fast as Grandma could make them. Mother smiled and thanked Pam for her help.

The sunrise was pouring light into the glass windows of the hut. Now was the time to straighten out their gear and put away clothes and personal items. Each woman had a cot for a bed and a few shelves next to it for her toothbrush, soap and washcloth. Pam realized with a pang there would be no showers for the entire time they were there. They would have to heat water on the stove for sponge baths, instead. She was really going to miss hot showers at home. She folded her sweaters and sweatshirts and stacked them in the shelves at the foot of the bed.

The cabin had a small dining table, one chair and a footstool. One of them would have to sit on a cot during meals.

At a small desk attached to a window, Mother was tinkering with the Osborne Fire Finder resting on a high stand in the center of the cabin. It was a sighting device aligned with a map of the area to help locate any smoke they might find. The idea was to pinpoint coordinates of a fire with the map of the Snoqualmie National Forest next to the big dial on the machine. She was lining them up. She needed to look around her territory and be ready to call in her report shortly.

Checking for smoke in all directions, she realized she might easily confuse the fog in the valleys with smoke from a fire. In an effort to help her, Pam darted down the steps to look around outside. Maybe she could tell her mother if she saw or smelled smoke. It was too early to see clearly, but she could help by raising the flag. She found it back inside the cabin and carried it to the flagpole. Enemy plane pilots should know they were there!

Pam heard Mother dial the number of the Enumclaw Ranger Station, give her name and lookout location name, and then say, "Nothing to report at this time." The telephone spokesman was friendly and made clear they were welcome at Suntop. "We didn't have anyone to cover it for the summer until you ladies stepped up," Pam heard her say. "We're glad y'all are going to be with us." All three of the Olmsted women grinned at the friendly message. This was going to be fun, and maybe they could count on help when they needed it.

As the days went by and afternoon temperatures heated up, gradually the snowbanks around the cabin melted away. Often they saw thunder clouds over distant mountains. Once Mother saw what she thought was the faraway smoldering start of a fire, a column of smoke. She called it in to the ranger district office and was embarrassed to learn that what she saw was a waterfall. "But it looked just like smoke," she protested.

Virginia Olmsted, Pam Olmsted (later Bobroff) and Lurline Simpson, another lookout and friend.

Pam Bobroff on the right, with Lurline Simpson.
Photos circa 1940 courtesy David Bobroff

The days grew warmer. Pam explored the trail and the meadows around Suntop's summit. They could see the closest fire lookout station on a nearby peak across the White River and foothills. Once in a while they heard the voice of that lookout calling in his reports, but there was no way they could see him in person from that distance. Not only did they not see or hear any enemy planes, but they didn't hear any planes at all.

Gray jays swooped by. Once one tried to land on her head. That made Pam laugh. Sometimes a raven would croak as it flew by, but mostly there was only the sound of wind and silence. Mount Rainier lost some of its white coat, and the heather in the meadows began to bloom a vivid pink color. Blue lupine and orange and magenta Indian paintbrush brightened up the meadow.

Pam made a friend out of a chipmunk she named "Chipper." He came around every day after breakfast looking for crumbs of the pancakes or cereal they had left over. She met him beside the steps to the cabin in a little hollowed out spot where she fed him. Pam loved feeding and talking to him, and he seemed to look only for her. Once he brought her a present—a piece of a broken gold bracelet that sparkled in the sum. She knew it was a present because he left it at the same place where she put his food. She thanked him with an extra big piece of toast.

One morning the clouds piled up over the Mountain in an unusual way. The District Ranger told them on the radio these were thunderheads, and that they should expect a thunder and lightning storm that afternoon. He advised them to come inside if the storm was close, and to stand on a stool or chair to divert the electricity. Mother, Grandma, and Pam were concerned. Could the lightning actually strike them? There was a lightning rod on the roof. How much protection would that be? They didn't know what to expect. There were not enough pieces of furniture where all three of them could stand if the lightning came close to Suntop Lookout.

Late on an afternoon that had been unusually hot and humid, the rain started. It was a pounding rain. Suddenly, they heard a distant thunderclap, and then another. The booms were getting closer together. Lightning flashed almost at the same time. The thunder was getting louder. Lightning seemed to light up the corners of the cabin. Pam wondered where was the safest place to go. Mother and Grandmother climbed on the stool and the chair, and Pam climbed on her cot. The storm thundered on and on. Mother screamed at her, "Don't be afraid, Pam." Lightning flashed in the closest trees. Of course she was afraid.

After more than half an hour, the storm moved on, and the rain stopped. The three women walked slowly down the cabin steps and gazed around them. A fire was burning in the tops of two alpine trees in the meadow. The trees had survived earlier forest fires and were slowly burning themselves out as she watched. The ground was soaked. No birds flew by and no winds rustled in the trees. The summit of Suntop was in shock.

"Chipper!" screamed Pam. What had happened to him? What if he had been killed by a lightning strike? She was half afraid to look for his body. She started to cry, convinced that he was gone. Mother thought he had hidden in a hole and told her he would come back in the morning.

They were too upset to make dinner. They munched on snacks the ranger had brought them. They called the Enumclaw Ranger Station to report they had survived a thunderstorm, but that they could not see any sign of a forest fire it had started. Other lookouts were undergoing the aftermath of the same storm, so the return message was a brief "Glad you're all right." Apparently thunderstorms were not unusual in this district. Pam felt as though she wanted to cry and cry for Chipper, but she knew she couldn't change whatever had happened to him.

Silently they went to bed, each woman thinking her own thoughts.

The next morning was clear and beautiful with bright sunshine. The sky was blue, and small fluffy clouds hovered over Mount Rainier. Pam ate a small breakfast and thought she would search for whatever was left of Chipper. She slowly walked down to his feeding place, dreading what she might find there.

But it was an impudent, hungry Chipper who waited for her. He looked cocky and glad to see her. "What have you got for me today?" he seemed to be saying. Pam burst into happy tears, saying his name over and over. "Chipper, Chipper, I love you."

****

Pam, her mother and grandmother also spent the summers of 1944 and 1945 serving as a lookout team on two other mountain lookouts. Happily, neither they nor any other lookouts in Washington State ever observed any enemy planes, though Pam and her family did report several small forest fires. After the war the men who had been soldiers returned to lookout duty. No women were assigned to watch for fires for many years. At the end of her life Pam remembered those beautiful summers on a lookout as "the best time of her life."

Three-generation lookout team on Suntop Mountain 1943.
Photo courtesy David Bobroff

VI

FOUNDER OF THE WASHINGTON TRAILS ASSOCIATION AND AUTHOR OF THE FIRST NORTHWEST HIKING GUIDE: LOUISE MARSHALL

Louise Marshall loved to hike. From the time she was a little girl in Boston she hiked, swam, paddled a canoe, rode horses and backpacked overnight. Her father was a doctor who thought girls should have the same opportunities as boys. He made sure his daughter did. She studied physical education and even got a Master's degree. Louise was good at all those activities

Before the Second World War Louise led several bicycle tours of Europe. While she was there with friends, she noticed people using guidebooks to find their way to trailheads. *Good idea!* thought Louise. She tucked the idea away for later.

After finishing her education, she wanted to go back to Europe, But the war was raging, so she couldn't go. Instead, she became a Baltimore teacher and met Bill Marshall, whom she married. They moved to Seattle. Louise wanted to explore the wonderful mountains she saw around her. The couple joined the Mountaineers, hoping to learn how to enjoy Northwest trails. When hike leaders were reluctant to tell a woman from the East Coast how to locate them, Louise offered to become a trail leader herself. Soon she was collecting trail information from other hike leaders. Like the European trip leaders she had observed, by the 1960s she had collected enough trip reports for a self-published soft covered little book *Trail Trips: An Introduction to Hiking Near Seattle*, one of the first trail guides in the region.

There were no smart phones or GPS guides then, so the book was valuable to hikers searching for directions to trailheads. She typed up the manuscript herself and had some copies made. She soon realized this was essential information. Hikers were eager for directions into the wilderness. So Louise started a newsletter she called *Signpost*. Every week she phoned hike leaders. took notes and combined them into current information on several pages. She and her daughters ran them off on a mimeograph (like a photocopier) machine in their barn, stapled, and addressed the *Signpost* letters by hand and mailed them out to subscribers who paid a small amount.

Hikers thanked her, but she realized the outdoor community needed a more detailed permanent guide than *Trail Trips,* which was easily damaged in a backpack. The Mountaineers had wanted to publish such a book. It seemed Louise was the perfect one to write it, and the famous Ira Spring agreed to take the pictures.

Well-used copy of cover of first hiking guide in Northwest by Louise Marshall. Original photo by Ira Spring

The book, *100 Hikes in Western Washington*, was the first official hike guidebook; it was enormously popular. Louise was proud of it and vowed to keep it updated when there was new information to be added. When she heard the Mountaineers were planning other regional hiking guides, listing 100 hikes in other areas, she thought she would be the one to write them.

But she was not. The Mountaineers chose another author, Harvey Manning, to write those books instead and she was passed over. Manning had written the first edition of *Mountaineering: The Freedom of the Hills* and was beloved in the hiking community. The 100 Hikes guidebook series sold for years, with Ira Spring doing the research and Harvey Manning writing up the descriptions from Ira's notes.

Louise wrote more guidebooks which she published herself. One was a guidebook to the Pacific Crest Trail, *High Trails*, which Mountaineers Books would not publish. She self-published it, marketing it through the *Signpost* newsletter. She also wrote *Winter Walks Near Seattle and Everett*. She always wondered why she was not asked to write the Mountaineers Books guidebooks. She wondered if it was because she was from the East Coast and a woman. No one would tell her.

She decided to devote more of her time to the environment and so she continued publishing *Signpost*. It became her voice. The newsletter developed into an advocacy outlet. She let her readers know if a land sale would destroy a trail, if lumber was being sold, or if roads needed to be improved. Notices of trail work parties began to be printed and volunteers began to organize.

Louise on a day hike in 1969. Her blue fanny pack contained her notebook and pencil for trailnotes, as well as her 35mm camera. All photos courtesy of the Marshall family collection.

Louise Marshall

Signpost magazine became the nonprofit Signpost Trails Association, which officially became the Washington Trails Association (WTA) in 1985. The WTA went on to offer its own trail maintenance program in 1993, carrying on the mission Louise had introduced. In addition to writing the guidebooks, newsletter publication and founding the WTA and the American Hiking Society, Louise was the first woman elected to REI's Board of Directors.

Louise lived to be 90. She saw her dreams of supporting trails and informing people about them come true. She believed trails should be accessible to everyone. Lovers of Northwest trails acknowledge that without her, many of the public lands we treasure today would not be available to us. When you visit the Washington wilderness and watch people of all ages access the trails, Louise Marshall comes to mind.

Her legacy is immense. It belongs to all of us.

JOAN FIREY, A NORTHWEST CLIMBING LEGEND

Joan Firey loved climbing Northwest mountains. In her lifetime she was a legend to other climbers because she was fearless. She explored unknown and unclimbed peaks. At the time little was known about those summits. Joan loved the challenge.

She didn't use a map or GPS because there were no maps of the area, and GPS had not yet been invented. Once she returned home from her ascents, she painted pictures of the glorious mountains she had climbed, so her admirers could see for themselves why she was passionate about them.

Joan grew up in California and met Joe Firey in 1949. They married and came to Seattle in the early 1950's. She was thin and wiry with short, curly reddish hair and the natural curiosity of an artist. Together they began to explore and climb. They identified the most difficult peaks in the Cascades, some of which had never been climbed. They started with the Picket Range in the North Cascades and the British Columbia Coast Range. Most climbers at that time had neither been there nor heard of them.

Joan Firey on a summit in the Selkirks, BC, 1950. Photo courtesy Carla Firey

Joan loved being the first person to reach a summit ---particularly if it was difficult to reach and spectacularly beautiful. When their three children were young, Joan and Joe would hire babysitters for two or three weeks at a time in order to be free to explore. Their daughter Carla felt left out, and so she grew up to be a climber too. She said, "I grew up in a Seattle household where reading contour maps was as normal as making a grocery list." (Contour maps have lines showing how high and how steep the mountains are.) Once Carla remembered a family friend telling her that "her mother was a true force of nature."

Despite their frequent absences, the Fireys were loving parents who found time to be active in their children's school communities and to help other families enjoy mountain hiking and camping. Joan was a physical therapist, as well as a painter. They took for granted the idea that "reasonable people might go places where they'd have to hike for days to get help if anyone became injured."

In 1960 the Fireys headed north to the Northern Pickets, where they made a first ascent of a new route on Mount Challenger. This mountain is known for its rugged rocky cliffs above massive glaciers. To climb it, Joan had to dig her axe deep and try not to look below. It took her a whole day to make the ascent.

She and Joe sometimes gave silly names to the peaks they climbed for the first time ever. Once they named a whole range the *Mustard Group*. They whimsically named its peaks and glacier for place names listed on a tube of Dijon mustard they carried in their packs to season their lunch crackers and salami. Their first ascents were of peaks they named *Ottohorn, Frenzel Spitz, Himmelgeisterhorn*, and *Dusseldorfspitz*. Even Fred Beckey, who wrote the climbing guide, laughed and left their peak names in his guidebook.

One by one they climbed the major summits of the Southern Pickets. Joan was proud to make the first ascent of the southeast peak of Mount Fury. In the BC Coast Range, they began with the Bella Coola Mountains, which are known for their dense forests and frequent rainfall. Unlike Phyllis Munday, who had to rely on a boat to get to the base of the peaks she wanted to climb, by the time Joan, Joe and their climbing friends went to the wilderness there were float planes, so they arrived by plane. That left them only a "mere seven hours of bumping, spine-jarring, dust biting, or mud wallowing, depending on the season," to reach the trailhead by four-wheel vehicle. To Joan it was all worth it. She didn't mind the discomfort one bit.

She loved climbing in mountains surrounding the Monarch Ice Field in Central BC. Most of the peaks there rise to between 8,500 and 10,000 feet, and Monarch stretches up to 11,000 feet. (Glaciers flow into immense sheets of ice called *ice fields*, much like waterfalls pour into a lake.)

Constant bad weather was an obstacle, but they took their chances and went anyway.

Monarch Icefield, oil painting. Joan Wilshire Firey, 1966. Copyright Carla Firey

In 1965 Joan, with Joe, made a first ascent and named The Citadel, a spectacular, difficult, and remote peak in Alaska. Eventually they climbed all the previously unexplored peaks in the Southern and Northern Pickets.

She and her friends began to venture on skis into the same beautiful areas in wintertime, taking a helicopter and overnight gear to the inaccessible areas. In 1977 she made a first winter ascent of Mount Terror, one of a team of four climbers, approaching the climb on foot. In July 1974 with her friend Piro Kramar she made a first ascent of a new route on Asperity Mountain in snow and ice conditions that were like winter. The mountain gets its name from the sharpness and severity of its summit.

By this time Joan had made 34 first ascents in the North Cascades and BC Coast Range. She had also climbed in Peru and Mexico, and she accompanied the Women's Himalayan Expedition to Annapurna, although she became ill and did not reach the summit.

Balfour Glacier, serigraph. J. Wilshire, 1970. Copyright Carla Firey

Joan Firey's watercolor and oil paintings reflect her love of the mountains. She called her work "Mountain Portraits." Her paintings tell us how she viewed the gorgeous mountains that called to her. Carla remembers her parents' profound belief that finding your way in uncertain terrain was one of the finer things in life. She also believes she was fortunate to grow up in a family that valued mountains as much as they did. Joan's legacy lives in her paintings of the mountains she loved.

Forbidden Cirque, oil on canvas. Joan Wilshire Firey, 1962. Copyright Carla Firey

Printed in the United States
by Baker & Taylor Publisher Services